NOT THIS PIG

NOT THIS PIG

POEMS BY

PHILIP LEVINE

WESLEYAN UNIVERSITY PRESS

Middletown, Connecticut

My thanks are given to the editors of the following publications in which many of these poems first appeared:

Paris Review; Encounter; Hudson Review; New York Review of Books; kayak; Mad River Review; Poetry Northwest; North American Review; New: Canadian & American Poetry; Intransit: Monster Issue, edited by Warhol and Malanga; and *Northwest Review.*

"Waking an Angel" was originally published in *Southern Review.*

"The Book" and "Spanish Lesson" were originally published in *Poetry.*

Lacking its first stanza, "The Cemetery at Academy, California" was originally published in *The New Yorker.*

Library of Congress Catalog Card Number: 68–16006

Manufactured in the United States of America

First printing February 1968; second printing May 1968

For Eddie mostly
& the cities that are here,
Detroit, Fresno, Barcelona

CONTENTS

NOT THIS PIG

I

COMING HOMEWARD FROM TOLEDO

We stopped at a beer garden,
drank, and watched the usual farmers
watching us, and gave a dull
country laborer a lift
in the wrong direction. He
giggled by the roadside where
we left him, pissing in snow
and waving, forty frozen
miles from home.

        When the engine
failed, we stood in a circle
of our breathing listening for
the sounds of snow.

        Later
just before the dawn of the
second day of a new year
already old, we found her
under white heaps, another
city in another time,
and fell asleep, and wakened
alone and disappointed
in a glass house under a
bare wood roof.

        I called out for
you, my brothers and friends, and
someone's children came, someone's
wife—puzzled helpful faces—
saying "father" and "husband."

You never answered, never
heard, under the frozen stars
of that old year where the snow
creaked in great mounds and the air
bronzed from the slag heaps twenty
miles south of Ecorse, for you were
happy, tired, and never going home.

IN A GROVE AGAIN

We stand in a grove where it's not snowing
with snow in our hair and on the tops of our shoes
    and along the life of the boughs that bring
forth the blossoms of snow. It's the life of poems:

    The blossoms are ceramic, fired, gold veined;
the boughs expensive; our feet dry. My companion,
    alas, is an underpaid Negro named
Eugene hired-on seven years ago at Dodge Main.

    He has the brain of a child, and he has a child
named Normandy who lives alone with her son.
    In short, his life is as boring as mine.
Meanwhile back in the car there are talismen:

    A heater, the splashed entrails of newspapers,
a speedometer that glows and always reads 0.
    We have not come here to die. We are workers
and have stopped to relieve ourselves, so we sigh.

A NEW DAY

The headlights fading out at dawn,
A stranger at the shore, the shore
Not wakening to the great sea
Out of sleep, and night, and no sun
Rising where it rose before.

The old champion in a sweat suit
Tells me this is Chicago, this—
He does not say—is not the sea
But the chopped grey lake you get to
After travelling all night

From Dubuque, Cairo, or Wyandotte.
He takes off at a slow trot
And the fat slides under his shirt.
I recall the Friday night
In a beer garden in Detroit

I saw him flatten Ezzard Charles
On TV, and weep, and raise
Both gloved hands in a slow salute
To a God. I could tell him that.
I could tell him that those good days

Were no more and no less than these.
I could tell him that I thought
By now I must have reached the sea
We read about, or that last night
I saw a man break down and cry

Out of luck and out of gas
In Bruce's Crossing. We collect
Here at the shore, the two of us,
To make a pact, a people come
For a new world and a new home

And what we get is what we bring:
A grey light coming on at dawn,
No fresh start and no bird song
And no sea and no shore
That someone hasn't seen before.

THE RATS

Because of the great press
of steel on steel
I cannot hear the shadows hunched
under the machines. When the power
fails, the machines stop,
and the lights go out
I am listening to myself,
to my breathing and to
the noise my breathing makes.

They are moving, the shadows,
out of time, out
of sight, somewhere out
there in the darkness, and
when the lights
come back they are no longer
where they were.

Someone who never stood
next to me has poisoned
the shadows. They are dead
in the stairwell or under
the floorboards, darker
than ever and more compact
and moving in the sweet air
sweetening the air I breathe.

Later I will be in
the parking lot looking
for my car or I will remember
I have no car and it
will be tomorrow or years
from then.

It will be now.
I will have been talking
sitting across from where
you sit at ease on
the outrageous, impeccable sofa
I have admired,
and in that quiet that comes
in speech I will hear them
moving at last and see them
moving toward you in the light
bringing their great sweetness.

THE BOOK

This muddy river consecrated
        by the soldiers who fouled it
in 1842 was forded

thirty years ago by the parents
        of Little Joe Rodríguez;
the book we are looking at they acquired

at great cost and through registered mail.
        It is deckled in gold,
and bound in leather, and substantial.

Someone has written with a fine pen
        and flaking gold ink across
the soldiers on the opposite bank

waiting to die. When I ask whose work
        it is, Little Joe blushes,
for it is his penmanship but his

father's anger encrusting the page.
        In the picture the soldiers
are Spaniards, he tells me in his strange

Shakespearean English, but the men
        who gave their poor lives to name
the river were Indians, uncles

and fathers of his father, their blood
        sold to heaven by a priest.
I wonder if he has ever said

so much at once and to a stranger,
        or if he speaks only when
his family abdicates the parlour.

It is evening, warm, the house is still
            and crowded with solitude.
He turns the page. A stone Robin Hood

rides a stone horse in the white plaza
            of the sun; he is no one's
father, no one's uncle, and his eyes—

blanker than the stone eyes of the horse—
            look forward to the future
where the men of the world sleep in peace.

COMMANDING ELEPHANTS

Lonnie said before this, "I'm
the chief of the elephants,
I call the tunes and they dance."
From his bed he'd hear the drum

of hooves in the bricked alley
and the blast of the Sheenie
calling for rags, wood, paper,
glass—all that was left over—

and from this he'd tell the time.
Beside the bed on a chair
the clean work pants, on the door
the ironed work shirt with his name,

and in the bathroom farther
than he could go the high-top
lace-up boots, the kind the scouts
wore and he'd worn since

he was twelve. To be asleep
hours after dawn, to have
a daughter in school when he
woke, a wife in the same shop

where he'd been the foreman
and said Go, where he'd tripped
the columns of switches and
brought the slow elephant feet

of the presses sliding down
in grooves as they must still do
effortlessly for someone.
"Oh my body, what have you

done to me?" he never said.
His hands surprised him; smelling
of soap, they lay at his sides
as though they were listening.

THE EVERLASTING SUNDAY

Waiting for it
in line to punch out
or punch in.
Bowed my head
into the cold grey
soup of the wash trough,
talked with men
who couldn't talk, marked
my bread with the black
print of my thumb
and ate it.

Nine-foot lengths
of alloy tubing between
my gloved hands
sliding, and the plop
of the cutter, and again
the tube drawing. Above
like swords, bundles
of steel sliding
in the blackened vaults,
and I, a lone child,
counting out.

Now to awaken,
pace the wood floor.
Through the torn shade
the moon between
the poplars riding
toward morning. My
dark suit, my stiffened
shirt stained
with God knows what,

my tie, my silvered
underwear guarding
the sad bed.

Naked, my hard arms
are thin as a girl's,
my body's hairs tipped
with frost. This house,
this ark of sleeping men,
bobs in the silence. I feel
my fingers curl
but not in anger,
the floor warms,
my eyes fill with light.
When was I young?

BLASTING FROM HEAVEN

The little girl won't eat her sandwich;
she lifts the bun and looks in, but the grey beef
    coated with relish is always there.
    Her mother says, "Do it for mother."
Milk and relish and a hard bun that comes off
    like a hat—a kid's life is a cinch.

    And a mother's life? "What can you do
with a man like that?" she asks the sleeping cook
    and then the old Negro who won't sit.
    "He's been out all night trying to get it.
I hope he gets it. What did he ever do
    but get it?" The Negro doesn't look,

    though he looks like he's been out all night
trying. Everyone's been out all night trying.
    Why else would we be drinking beer
    at attention? If she were younger,
or if I were Prince Valiant, I would say that fate
    brought me here to quiet the crying,

    to sweeten the sandwich of the child,
to waken the cook, to stop the Negro from
    bearing witness to the world. The dawn
    still hasn't come, and now we hear
the 8 o'clock whistles blasting from heaven,
    and with no morning the day is sold.

II

ABOVE IT ALL

Strapped to my seat, I turn
to the thin Air Force major
and ask how far to L.A.
He lifts his sunglasses, stares
down at the ocean slipping
beneath, and says, "50 minutes."
We've left the land behind us,
the stump-pocked crests, the creased hills
of Vandenberg Missile Base
where nothing moved, nothing breathed
except one lone steam engine
pulling nothing, and the waves
which came at the shore as though
they mattered, row after row.

The major reads; his lips move
soundlessly, wordlessly
like a lunatic's in love,
he reads that they're making us
get out of our cars to be
counted, they're getting tough
and we're getting tougher back,
he passes over the small
blurred photo of Jean Cocteau,
the names of the champions
Cerdan, LaMotta, Piaf,
for whom there are no poems.
If I shut my eyes I know
I'll be in a private home
for the blind where things are worse.

My good neighbor, the major,
looks at me. His eyes are young,
placid, and light blue as though
unused, and he offers me
half his newspaper, offers
his window seat—for he's seen
it all—offers a comment
on the weather but not on
the night which seems to be
gathering at the margins
of sight or the bottom
of the ocean or in
the twin periods marking
the dead centers of our eyes.

OBSCURE

She has hidden in a box
the dearest part of herself.
She has sealed its face with wax
so that the lips cannot part,
nor the tongue move, nor the voice
cry out for help, but the heart—
she feels sure—must be beating
like the pulse of a wren or
the eyes of a spotted hare.

She is having tea. Someone,
a man, bends by the fire . . .
No, no, that will be later
or never, for first she must
sit still in a workingman's
bar in Calwa, just under
the raised television set
where her shot glass has lain down
in a puddle. She has seen

so much, and knows so little.
She does not want to hurry,
but if she does not find it
she will not ever marry,
or worse, she will not mother.
Oh, but she is wrong. She will
mother many, and their names
will be those of scholarships,
civic children, and white hopes,

their names will be all her names
and she will know they are real
reading them in the evening
during station breaks. The wall
between her and the old game
of hide-and-seek thickens like
soaped glass, and now she cannot
turn away or be frantic.
Her eyes run. She is obscure.

BARBIE & KEN, KEN & BARBIE

Ken has a big job at Castle Air Force Base
where the work is challenging and the future
lies on the cutting room table, docile and clear
for Ken, who with scissors unwrinkles its face.

Ken drives to Paso Robles on the weekend
in a sports car that runs on needle bearings;
he takes the turns hard and as he does he sings
for up ahead is the ocean and the sand

and Barbie in a pink negligee, Barbie
waiting in her tall pink pumps, golf clubs ready.
The coast hills are greener than they used to be,
the ocean restless, only Ken is steady.

Soon they'll be together, brother and sister,
Barbie and Ken, sharing a toothbrush, sharing
a toilet, a tub, sharing the same old song
that freezes on their lips, sharing each other

for that breathless moment when the elders
bow to their credit card. Sundays would be hell
what with packing, parting, and the long haul
if brother and sister weren't such good soldiers.

FAMILY PLAN

The word was that we were getting out
    so at dawn in the burned field
across from where we'd tried to live
    we gathered our utensils
and tried to look like soldiers or tried
    to look as though we believed
that someone might be afraid of us.
    There were small white clouds turning
toward the rim of heat. I imagined
    the road we would take, the sudden
swaths of daisies bowing to the road

and the bees exploding before us
    before we could flinch. I put
all this in the past tense although it's
    happening now, but how else
can I make you believe? If I said
    that the ashes in the hair
of my youngest son make him look like
    a new God born out of fire
would you think I was nuts? If I said,
    "The car starts, the tank is full,
and yet we are not going to leave,"
    would it make any difference?

POSSESSION

They thought they could go back
to find the same marked squirrels
nesting in the walnut trees
and that there would be some work
to do, something useful
and hard, and that they might please

their own need to be doing.
You know what they found. They found
themselves standing in your yard
awed by the gladiolus
and the absence of something
they knew. This had been free land,

they said, but now it was yours
who went in to call the law.

TO A CHILD TRAPPED IN A BARBER SHOP

You've gotten in through the transom
    and you can't get out
till Monday morning or, worse,
    till the cops come.

That six-year-old red face
    calling for mama
is yours; it won't help you
    because your case

is closed forever, hopeless.
    So don't drink
the Lucky Tiger, don't
    fill up on grease

because that makes it a lot worse,
    that makes it a crime
against property and the state
    and that costs time.

We've all been here before,
    we took our turn
under the electric storm
    of the vibrator

and stiffened our wills to meet
    the close clippers
and heard the true blade mowing
    back and forth

on a strip of dead skin,
            and we stopped crying.
You think your life is over?
            It's just begun.

WHO ARE YOU?

It's morning; you are six,
Impatient to be off
In the clear cold light
Of the second week in March.

I'm your father in
Whose grasp you can't hold still.
Your brother calls; it's time
To leave for kindergarten,

But I must wax your cowlick,
Brush your hair down,
Button your starched collar
And make sure you have your folder.

I let you go a mess
Knowing that you'll cry
If he should call again.
I am left alone

Hearing the front door close,
You and your older brother
Setting off together
Across the wet lawns.

Where will you arrive?
And will I know you then,
Blue-eyed and American?
"Grandma is Jewish," you said

At Christmas time. What will
You say to me when you
Are taunted as a Jew?
Or do they do such things

In the new glass school?
As though they ever stop.
It's 9; the buzzer sounds;
Miss Jennings has you now;

You stand beside your desk,
Pledge your flag and sing
Slightly out of tune
"For spacious fields of grain."

Are you of no people
Punished for their God?
You'd answer laughing, "Here
Is the church, there is the steeple."

You live for Easter now,
With colored eggs and bunnies,
Everyone's vacation,
And Sunday brings the funnies.

Wondering who you are,
Wondering what unknown fathers
Have reached through me to you,
I turn to the cold mirror

To see your face in mine,
My father's face as well,
As well as I remember.
Marked with the mark of Cain

Somewhere beyond the Flood
We wandered hand in hand
In a country we remember
Somewhere in our blood,

Homeless we three and certain
Of who we were. Your face
Is older now you are
No longer here, your hair

Is darker and your eyes
Are wide and full with tears
And your father is
Your father and no more.

THE ONE-EYED KING

At last I found and faced you there.
My two eyes fixed a steady eye
In the kingdom of necessity.
Heavy with the true despair

That comes from finding what you are,
I bowed and said "My God" to you,
And you bowed as you lately do
And held your peace. It's almost here—

The day on which our guts will billow
Like mattress stuffing, our lungs blow
Like ashes, and the shapes go;
So rest awhile on the pillow

Of this tired thigh, rest and begin
To shrivel back where you began,
Where some old idiot said the man
In all his glory sheds this skin.

THE RECEIVER

I waken with the television on
And no one here. It's Sunday afternoon,
The phone was ringing but it's silent now;
Only the television and the sun,

Which burns along my arm, have been awake.
This is impossible. There is no phone,
Only a play receiver in my hand,
An unconnected one, efficient, black,

That always gets its man. I dial you
And listen to the customary rings,
And then more rings and more until I know
That everything suspected must be true.

I hang up and unscrew the listening piece.
What would you have me find so close to home?
A Chinese message or a little man?
Or a small mirror that refused my face?

The surprise was that there was nothing there,
Nothing at all, nothing, not even ought,
And thus it was that in my 35th year
I learned that by these words I hid my thought.

THE HOUSE OF THE HANGED CHILD

The clouds have not gathered today.
It is April, and the white house
drops a black shadow. The three men
in their stiff vests are listening;
you can tell by the way the porch
with its flaking pillars
keeps them apart.

                    They have no songs,
no radios in the electric morning.
Their hair has coarsened; their lips,
their brows and hands have darkened
in the frame of white America.
They are becoming
speechless, they are becoming
Portuguese.

                    The television echoes
behind them from room to room.
Sand settles in the bare wood halls.
The house will not let them in.
Near the cypresses shading the white
Impala no one can drive
a small dark brother leans
toward the freeways and the music,
burning like a hive of tears.

THE CEMETERY AT ACADEMY, CALIFORNIA

On a hot summer Sunday
I came here with my children
who wandered among headstones
kicking up dust clouds. They found
a stone that said DAVI and
nothing more, and beneath the stone
a dead gopher, flat and dry.
Later they went off to play
on the dry dirt hills; I napped
under a great tree and woke
surprised by three teenagers.
They had put flowers in tin cans
around a headstone that showed
the sunrise over a slate sea,
and in the left-hand corner
a new bronze dove broke for peace.
Off in the distance my boys
had discovered the outhouses,
the twin white-washed sentinels,
and were unwinding toilet
paper and dropping whatever
they could find through the dark holes,
and when I found and scolded
them the two younger ones squeezed
my hands and walked stiffly at
my side past the three mourners.

I came here with a young girl
once who perched barefoot on her
family marker. "I will go
there," she said, "next to my sister."
It was early morning and
cold, and I wandered over
the pale clodded ground looking
for something rich or touching.

"It's all wildflowers in the spring,"
she had said, but in July
there were only the curled cut
flowers and the headstones blanked out
on the sun side, and the long
shadows deep as oil. I walked
to the sagging wire fence
that marked the margin of the
place and saw where the same ground,
festered here and there with reedy
grass, rose to a small knoll
and beyond where a windmill
held itself against the breeze.
I could hear her singing on
the stone under the great oak,
but when I got there she was
silent and I wasn't sure
and was ashamed to ask her,
ashamed that I had come here
where her people turned the earth.

Yet I came again, alone,
in the evening when the leaves
turned in the heat toward darkness
so late in coming. There was
her sister, there was her place
undisturbed, relatives and
friends, and other families
spread along the crests of this
burned hill. When I kneeled
to touch the ground it seemed like
something I had never seen,
the way the pale lumps broke down
to almost nothing, nothing
but the source of what they called
their living. She, younger now
than I, would be here some day

beneath the ground my hand combed.
The first night wind caught the leaves
above, crackling, and on
the trunk a salamander
faded in the fading light.
One comes for answers to a
place like this and finds even
in the darkness, even in
the sudden flooding of the
headlights, that in time one comes
to be a stranger to nothing.

SILENT IN AMERICA

"Vivas for those who have failed . . . "

I

Since I no longer speak I
go unnoticed among men;
in the far corners of rooms,
greeted occasionally
with a stiff wave, I am seen
aslant as one sees a pane

of clear glass, reflecting both
what lies before and behind
in a dazzle of splendid
approximations. They mouth
to each other, and the wind
answers them, while my tongue, furred,

captive, wandering between
contagious wards of the palate,
discovers a foreignness
that is native. One woman,
hearing me grunt for breath, sits
by my side in a green dress,

her hands cupped in the valley
of her life. She would receive
my sympathy and in my
eyes sees—God knows what she sees
in my eyes. Let them have
all they find under the sky.

II

Sometimes on especially
    warm evenings I
take a card chair out under
    the almond tree

and catching the last light, speak
    to myself without
words. I try to catch what is
    behind my throat,

without words, all that exists
    behind and before.
Under the low branches the
    earth's matted floor,

cropped Bermuda and clover
    that the bees attack,
glistens in shade. The sprinkler
    swings out of dark

into light and back again,
    and the water sighs
as though it were suffering
    before my own eyes.

Before my own eyes I am
    almost speaking; my
jaws ache for release, for
    words that will say

anything. I force myself
    to remember
who I am, what I am, and
    why I am here.

III
When Dr. Leo
addresses me, I pretend
to be distracted:
"Look here, Philip, no
damage," and he points his wand
at a clogged bridge-head

in the white-on-black
map of my throat. The lights come
on again. I blink
like a good patient.
Behind two great stained thumbs
he advances straight

toward my defenseless
mouth, enters and pries. The hair
on his hands interests
me no longer, nor
does his magic power amaze.
He has his good days

and his bad. I see
from her gold breast-pin nursey's
a grade A typist,
and he, from his acts,
is an existentialist
with no faith in facts.

IV
And I, I am the silent
riser in a house
of garrulous children.
I am Fresno's

dumb bard, America's last
        hope, sheep in sheep's
clothing. Who names the past
        names me, who sleeps

by my side shall find despair
        and happiness,
a twi-night double header.
        He who loves less

than I, loves no one, who speaks
        more than I, speaks
too much. I am everything
        that is dishonest,

everything under the sun.
        And I say "balls,"
the time will never come
        nor ripeness be all.

v

        I tell time
by the sunlight's position
        on the bedroom wall:
it's 5:30, middle June.
        I rise, dress,
        assume my name

        and feel my
face against a hard towel.
        My mind is empty;
I see all that's here to see:
        the garden
        and the hard sky;

the great space
between the two has a weight,
    a reality
which I find is no burden,
        and the height
        of the cot tree

    is only
what it has come to deserve.
    I have not found peace,
but I have found I am where
        I am by
        being only there,

    by standing
in the clouded presence of
    the things I observe.
What is it in the air or the
        water caught
        on the branches

    of the brown
roses hanging toward autumn?
    What is it that moves
when it's still, and strikes me dumb
        when it speaks
        of being alive.

VI

In a room with no way out,
abandoned by everyone
to something they call my fate,
with only my squat demon,
my little Bobby, jumping up
and down, demanding women,

demanding more in his cup,
pushing his hand where a hand

should not be pushed, pushing his
shrill voice everywhere, I tried
escape, but the broken stairs
went nowhere. "Police," I cried,
but the phones were off the hook,
and I wasn't, and Bobby
was close behind with a trick
or two up his sleeve, his fly

catching like canvas on the
night wind, crying, "One more, just one."
Knowing he would master me,
I turned to you: "Levine,"
I called softly, and called you
again and again, and it was I who,
given unto Bobby, screamed NO.

VII

    For a black man whose
name I have forgotten who danced
    all night at Chevy
        Gear & Axle,
    for that great stunned Pole
who laughed when he called me Jew
    Boy, for the ugly
        who had no chance,

    the beautiful in
body, the used and the unused,
    those who had courage
        and those who quit—
    Rousek and Ficklin

numbed by their own self-praise
who ate their own shit
in their own rage;

for these and myself
whom I loved and hated, I
had presumed to speak
in measure.
The great night is half
over, and the stage is dark;
all my energy,
all my care for

those I cannot touch
runs on my breath like a sigh;
surely I have failed.
My own wife
and my children reach
in their sleep for some sure sign,
but each has his life
private and sealed.

VIII
I speak to H. in a bar
in downtown L.A.
Over a schooner of beer
he waits out the day
in the anonymous dark.
Archimbault is here—
I do not have to be drunk
to feel him come near,

and he touches me with his
life, and I could cry,
though I don't know who he is

or why I should care
about the mad ones, imagined
    and real, H. places
in his cherished underground,
    their wounded faces

glowing in the half-light of
    their last days alive,
as his glows here. Let me have
    the courage to live
as fictions live, proud, careless,
    unwilling to die.
We pay for our drinks, rise,
    and enter the city

waiting, impatient and loud.
    Come with us tonight,
drifters in the drifting crowd,
    we shall arrive, late
and tired, beyond the false lights
    of Pasadena
where the living are silent
    in America.

THE MORNING AFTER THE STORM

I

In my neighbor's yard
the wrecked cars dream
of the heli-arc and the pop
of the rubber mallet.

He is a capitalist
in bodywork, even his
tin shed sweats
and says " 'aftanoon,"

and tolerates
my nigger guests.
It's a good land:
May the water rise

from nowhere
under a calm sky
and quiet his tools
and soften his hands.

II

His little brow is wet,
his hair is wet; his eyes,
set wide apart like a dog's,
open and he smiles.

Outside the stunted sycamore
is growling in the last
stains of the dawn.
Light chips at the branches,

and the winter birds
stutter into the day.
He rises and stands
under the bulb, naked,

takes his shorts, socks,
pants, piece by piece,
blinking into his eyes
the colorless light.

He forgives me
everything and hurries
through milk and cornflakes
not to be late.

Skips into the day.
I crouch, breathless,
on his bed, and smell
his sleeping terror.

III

The winds and the dogs
brought down the garbage.
Ostrichlike, my wife picks
at the tidbits on the lawn.

The wet winds gust,
and her night clothes flap around her—
in her 40th year
she stoops and pecks and clears

our little yard;
she turns away from nothing,
grounds, bottles, bones,
egg shells, animal fat,

the splintered plastic guns,
the burned-out bulbs
and swollen batteries,
all the refuse of this house.

The sky clenches again.
Our three sons grow toward war.
Child of the land, Indian,
you cannot live here any more.

VISITING DAY

Barcelona, 1965

On the way out we laugh, children
going to our Sunday picnic,
and the Spaniards laugh, for they
have nothing to do with the death
of the world.
                    The sea is blue, blue
and nothing else; when the waves break
they break into blue.
                    The carrier
rises like a cross, and we come
to it as the waves come to it,
breaking themselves against the hull;
our launch knocks and knocks; it opens,
and we ascend. I am climbing
to the life of my children.
I smile, friendly and glad to be
among my people.
                    A pilot
shows us his own attack bomber;
he is like a painter speaking
the language of machines; his hands
trace in the air, and his eyes bathe
in the late light. Does he come
knocking in his sleep, shorn of wings,
and crying?
                    After milk and cake
we go back under the shadow
of the *FDR* toward the harbor,

while the sea is turning over,
turning in its sleep, turning to us
all at once its burned face.

YO SOY AMERICANO

He tells me in Spanish worse than mine.
It has been raining, and it will rain
again; our cars, side by side,

are being attended to like Catholics:
here in La Mancha tiny lackeys
in uniform fill them

with Texaco. We are in Wyoming;
the windmills, the silent pueblos
the color of beans will fold up

as soon as the movie is over.
He tells me he's an American,
this time in French. His Corvair

is filled, with clothes, records, tables, lamps.
He could be. He could be St. Augustine
looking for pear trees in Spain.

He could be someone out of my life
hiding in a long Belgian overcoat
and a hard Belgian accent.

He hates me. It's 20 years after;
he's the brown son of a black bridge-builder
who will die in Chicago,

and I'm in a Volkswagen with three
blue-eyed kids eating oranges. We
keep our hands in our pockets.

IN SAXONY

A little girl with blond braids
waved from behind the barricade.
I answered. We were smiling.

The only noise was the train
slipping on oiled rails, and the sun
snapping through the poplar boughs.

We were going. No burned-out cars,
no tumbled field of oil drums
at the town's end, only a man

in a peaked grey cap, waving.
When he lit a cigarette
with a square, stainless lighter

I could see the egg of flame
in the still air, I could feel
it burning through the last wall

into my mind, I could smell
my own mind like singed hair.
How could it happen here?

THE MIDGET

In this café Durruti,
the unnamable, plotted
the burning of the Bishop
of Zaragoza, or so
the story goes. Now it's a hot
tourist spot in season, but
in mid-December the bar
is lined with factory workers
and day laborers as grey
as cement. The place smells
of cement and of urine,
and no one takes off his coat
or sits down to his sherry—
a queen's drink, as thin and dry
as benzine.
             It is Sunday,
late, and each man drinks alone,
seriously. Down the bar
a midget sings to himself,
sings of how from the starving South
he came, a boy, to this terrible
Barcelona, and ate. Not
all the songs are for himself;
he steps back from the bar,
his potbelly pushed out
and wrapped intricately
in a great, somber cummerbund,
and tells the world who is big,
big in the heart, and big down
here, big where it really counts.

Now he comes over to me,
and it is for me he sings.
Does he want money? I try
to buy him off with a drink,

a bored smile, but again
I hear of his power, of how
the Germans, Dutch, English—all
the world's babies—come to him,
and how on the fields of skin
he struts. "Here," he says to me,
"feel this and you'll believe."

In a voice suddenly thin
and adolescent, I tell him
I believe. "Feel this, feel this . . . "
I turn away from him, but
he turns with me, and the room
freezes except for us two.
I can smell the bitterness
of his sweat, and from the cracked
corners of his eyes see the tears
start down their worn courses.
I say, No, No more! He tugs
at my sleeve, hulking now, and
too big for his little feet;
he tugs and will not let go,
and the others along the bar
won't turn or interfere
or leave their drinks. He gets
my hand, first my forefinger
like a carrot in his fist,
and then with the other hand,
my wrist, and at last I can't
shake him off or defend
myself.
            He sits in my lap
and sings of Americas,
of those who never returned
and those who never left. The smell

of anise has turned his breath
to a child's breath, but his cheeks,
stiff and peeling, have started
to die. They have turned along
the bar to behold me
on the raised throne of a torn
plastic barstool, blank and drunk
and half asleep. One by one
with the old curses thrown down
they pay up and go out,
and though the place is still
except for the new rumbling
of the morning catching fire
no one hears or no one cares
that I sing to this late-born freak
of the old world swelling my lap,
I sing lullaby, and sing.

THE CARTRIDGES

You sleep weightless on my palm, the revolver
I smuggled across eleven borders
hidden in my raincoat, hidden from my wife,
my children, myself. But now we are

alone with the radio and its cries
in the off-season villa by the shore,
so into this chapel of banalities
I give you my hand, I give you my life.

Six little .22 long-rifle slugs
golden-haloed like guardian angels,
their glum faces grease-smeared, are on the table
posed on a sheet of pure typing paper.

At home in California in my rifle,
closeted now and bandaged in a torn sheet,
they would mean nothing, the final opening
of a rabbit brain, the release of clichés,

the release of gases, animal pain,
or the tearing of glass. Nothing at all.
Here in my numbed fingers, one by one,
I take them up and give them to their stations.

First you, my little American, you bring
reports of everything I left behind,
and you, the hope of middle age, the game
I play with sleep when sleep is everything.

And you, stupid, are a black hole in the air
and nothing more. I refuse to explain.
And you, all of whose names are simply Spain,
are every pure act I don't dare.

This one has no name and no nation
and has been with me from the start. And you,
finally, you have a name I will not name, a face
I cannot face, you could be music, you

could be the music of snow on the warm plain
of Michigan, you could be my voice
calling to me at last, calling me out of Spain,
calling me home, home, home, at any price.

SPANISH LESSON

For Juan R. and his father,
with Machado at the end

We look down into a garden
of spines as the evening gathers
in the shadows of the new wall.
The blank stone terrace has no rail,
and I feel I could walk in air.
"Rosemary, cactus, sweet basil . . . "
It is night, and he is naming
the gems of his captive garden
like Ophelia or like the God
he no longer allows.
      Inside,
behind glass, the little heater
glows with electric warmth. We sit
and resume the lesson, but it won't
go. The wind is catching in the eaves,
and the garden bangs in his ears,
and beyond the garden the lost wars
and the lost poets, and the names
of the defeats blessed by saints
at the Ebro, the Llobregat,
the Guadalquivir.
      His brows
are like twin, stiff arches above
his eyes, but he is not surprised—
nothing in himself is surprised—
and the jaw's latent movement
is without fear, and the shadows
along the jaw are without fear.

He is starting to die, to die
of care and of the need to be read
even as I read him, a rhythm
only, stumbling and American.

THE BUSINESSMAN OF ALICANTE

He's on my front porch rapping
        like a woodpecker.
No, he will not come in,

this man from Alicante;
        he wants a moment
to unravel the White Coast

from his carved suitcase, "the first
        garden of the world,"
and he points his forefinger

to heaven, May it witness!
        I can buy all this,
the garden, and the children

of the garden, and he winks.
        The towers, the cliffs,
the unchanging blue of sky

and sea tumble through his hands
        all out of focus.
No, I say, this is not my land.

Oh, but it is, he insists,
        and the forefinger
bears witness. It is the last

garden of the world, the last
        slip of land breaking
into the sea, the last crust

of earth we will chew before
        water is our bread.
I don't understand a word.

But I must, he says, and winks
        and winks and won't speak
English and won't be serious.

I go in and slam the door
        and leave him standing
and don't look to see if he's there.

I can hear him, waiting.
        I can hear my breath,
and then the damp chill the day

will pass into and then
        the trees darkening
like clusters of frightened wrens.

WINTER RAINS, Cataluña

I

The Pegasos are steaming
in the rain like scared horses,
and the horses gasp and gasp
to hold their scalding treasures.

Mules, donkeys, women in black,
men in plastic envelopes,
all the unread messages to God
that one cop holds back.

Leathered, gauntleted, and armed;
when the light falls his halo
begins to pulse, and his eyes
behind blank goggles see no

evil they can't master, no
hidden feature they can't place.
The white sword of his raised arm
drops like justice, and we go.

II

His right side drags under the weight
of his tommy gun. He lifts the sling
with his thumb; it is habit,
it is the shrug of a silent man

under the weight of everything.
We stand beneath a tree, side by side,
like two men at a bar, facing the mirror
of the world, he the warrior

with a corked and rusting weapon,
and I the child who has never killed.
Mother is cross. Her boys are huddled
and stamping out in the dark rain.

III

Waiting to go out
I stand with my coat
but the rain doesn't stop.
A lake grows in my street.

Up the hill the rents grow
and the waters pour down. The moans
of the drowned stall and start
and stall like a mule cart.

And seen from above
even the sea is abstract,
that corner of his art
which bears the signature.

IV

The unfinished wall
keeps to itself
like a wounded mountain.
The air is unsafe.

Birds are holding
themselves with their brothers,
the stones; they breathe
like carburetors

and glisten in the late light.
The stones have shut
their eyes; if it is night,
if it is the long sigh

of dynamite,
if it is too late
to huddle in flooded cellars
they don't care.

v

In March these fields of nettles
will bear a white scum,
the sour afterthought of heaven,
and the pinpoints of wildflowers

will sprout from nowhere
like the late blossoming
of saints. By a rotting shed,
untethered now, a horse bows

under the fine whippings of rain.
The fields float in his eyes,
the battered arks of husks
spinning and bobbing all day,

until the sky darkens and calms,
and calms the surface of these waters,
weighs down and calms his eyes,
and spreads their darkness like a sigh.

V

HEAVEN

If you were twenty-seven
and had done time for beating
your ex-wife and had
no dreams you remembered
in the morning, you might
lie on your bed and listen
to a mad canary sing
and think it all right to be
there every Saturday
ignoring your neighbors, the streets,
the signs that said join,
and the need to be helping.
You might build, as he did,
a network of golden ladders
so that the bird could roam
on all levels of the room;
you might paint the ceiling blue,
the floor green, and shade
the place you called the sun
so that things came softly to order
when the light came on.
He and the bird lived
in the fine weather of heaven;
they never aged, they
never tired or wanted
all through that war,
but when it was over
and the nation had been saved,
he knew they'd be hunted.
He knew, as you would too,

that he'd be laid off
for not being braver,
and it would do no good
to show how he had taken
clothespins and cardboard
and made each step safe.
It would do no good
to have been one of the few
that climbed higher and higher
even in time of war,
for now there would be the poor
asking for their share,
and hurt men in uniforms,
and no one to believe
that heaven was really here.

SUNDAY AFTERNOON

At first when we saw a girl
hit with a beer can and saw
one so drunk he wet his pants,
we moved back and gave them room,
and what mattered was to be
unnoticed.

                On the body
of the Angel without teeth
I counted seventeen welts
scored with a bicycle chain.
Another was hunched into
the shape clay might take if it
were battered with pine boughs,
and the third who ran off down
a fire trail crying, "I am King
of Richmond," returned like dirt
in the bed of a pick-up.

This was Sunday afternoon
in America, the quiet
daydream of the Sierras,
the celebrations the land
demands. We left the cold fires
of the barbecue, we left
our homes grumbling in the heat
like beached U-boats and came by two's
or with the kids up the long
black cut of highway to see
the first great movies made flesh.

BY ANIMALS, BY MEN, AND BY MACHINES

The doctor, he tells me, is a "nice nigger,"
      the nurses are all unfuckable,
even the tight-assed one who calls him Sugar.

What a hell of a place to be, and the sun
      catches the steel screw in the center
of his right eye, and he gleams like a small coin.

He sees that I see, and raises himself on
      one elbow and whispers, "It's spooky."
I smell the dust in his yellow beard, the gin

on his breath, which may be ether, and something
      which is his and has never been touched—
not even by the horn in his eye, or the slug

smearing out half his teeth and mangling his tongue,
      or the cycle wheel corkscrewing his foot.
When I leave the ward he will begin to sing

of the Yellow River or the Red River
      while the public hands of the doctor
grope toward the pain. They will tell him they must save

his life and take his leg, or save his leg and
      take his life; from table to table
he'll fly without drugs; they'll pass him from hand

to hand while he dreams above them on the horn
      of a steer or snaps in the flaming air
above his cycle, singing that he was born.

WAKING AN ANGEL

Sparrows quarreled outside our window,
roses swelled, the cherry boughs burst
into fire, and it was spring

in the middle of a bad winter.
We have been good, she said, we have
avoided the fields, tended

our private affairs without complaint,
and this is surely our reward.
I wasn't so sure. There were

hard grey spots on the underbelly
of the ring-tailed coon that died
in the garbage, there was sand

as white as powdered glass overflowing
the vessel of the hyacinth,
there was sand on my own tongue

when I awakened at one or two
in the dark, my nostrils inflamed,
my voice crying out for her.

She wouldn't move. I put my cold hands
on her hips and rocked her gently;
O, O, O was all she said

through set, dry lips. She was slipping
away from me. I was afraid to look
at what dense wings lifted her

out of my bedroom and my one life,
her voice still trailing O, O, O,
like a raiment of victory.

THE SECOND ANGEL

We could be going home.
He sits behind me. The road
breaks over the charred crests
and I follow. I want to speak.
I hear his lips and fingers
meeting in the drained rhythms
of prayer, I hear the pages
fluttering like the voices
of farm wives, like the voices
of onions. Is it money?
He could buy it all, harvests
of dried-out, cured cars, vineyards
of ashes.
                    Along the road
the burned gangs of small drawn men
explode into peonies.
In the mirror his face grows—
ancient and smooth and raised,
a face that has never cried,
a face of growing stone, a face
as cold as newsprint. This angel
is my brother. When I turn
he sees all my madness, all
my anger. He sees I'm lost
forever.
              The body is
light as milk, and still I bruise
his head against the doorpost,
and carry him, calm and pliant,
and lay him in the roadside
bones and nettles like a doll,
his eyes still open, seeing,
his wings breathing in and out
in the winds of traffic. What
can I do but turn away,

my chest and arms smeared with dust
and tipped with bloodless feathers.
My brother, the angel, has fallen.

THE LOST ANGEL

Four little children
in winged costumes—
it has something to do

with raising money.
Children are hungry
the one says, the one

who can talk.
And they go down the drive
in the driving rain, and there's

no car
to collect them, no
one waiting, and the bills

and coins spill
from his trailing hand
and float like pieces of light.

Wait! Wait!
I yell, and run
to gather what I can,

and he turns,
the one who can talk,
holding his empty fists

as offerings,
two shaking hammers,
and gives me back my life.

ANIMALS ARE PASSING FROM OUR LIVES

It's wonderful how I jog
on four honed-down ivory toes
my massive buttocks slipping
like oiled parts with each light step.

I'm to market. I can smell
the sour, grooved block, I can smell
the blade that opens the hole
and the pudgy white fingers

that shake out the intestines
like a hankie. In my dreams
the snouts drool on the marble,
suffering children, suffering flies,

suffering the consumers
who won't meet their steady eyes
for fear they could see. The boy
who drives me along believes

that any moment I'll fall
on my side and drum my toes
like a typewriter or squeal
and shit like a new housewife

discovering television,
or that I'll turn like a beast
cleverly to hook his teeth
with my teeth. No. Not this pig.

BABY VILLON

He tells me in Bangkok he's robbed
Because he's white; in London because he's black;
In Barcelona, Jew; in Paris, Arab:
Everywhere and at all times, and he fights back.

He holds up seven thick little fingers
To show me he's rated seventh in the world,
And there's no passion in his voice, no anger
In the flat brown eyes flecked with blood.

He asks me to tell all I can remember
Of my father, his uncle; he talks of the war
In North Africa and what came after,
The loss of his father, the loss of his brother,

The windows of the bakery smashed and the fresh bread
Dusted with glass, the warm smell of rye
So strong he ate till his mouth filled with blood.
"Here they live, here they live and not die,"

And he points down at his black head ridged
With black kinks of hair. He touches my hair,
Tells me I should never disparage
The stiff bristles that guard the head of the fighter.

Sadly his fingers wander over my face,
And he says how fair I am, how smooth.
We stand to end this first and last visit.
Stiff, 116 pounds, five feet two,

No bigger than a girl, he holds my shoulders,
Kisses my lips, his eyes still open,
My imaginary brother, my cousin,
Myself made otherwise by all his pain.